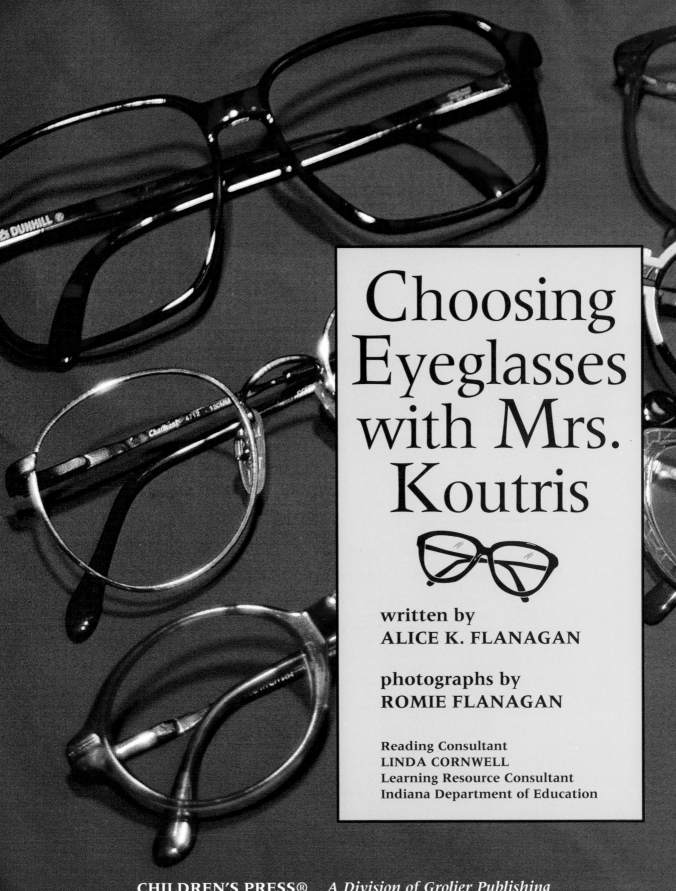

Choosing Eyeglasses with Mrs. Koutris

written by
ALICE K. FLANAGAN

photographs by
ROMIE FLANAGAN

Reading Consultant
LINDA CORNWELL
Learning Resource Consultant
Indiana Department of Education

CHILDREN'S PRESS® *A Division of Grolier Publishing*
New York • London • Hong Kong • Sydney • Danbury, Connecticut

*Special thanks to Linda Koutris
for allowing us to tell her story.*

Also, thanks to Dr. May and Deerfield Optical.

Author's Note:

Mrs. Koutris's last name is pronounced KOOTRIS.

Library of Congress Cataloging-in-Publication Data

Flanagan, Alice.

    Choosing eyeglasses with Mrs. Koutris / written by Alice K. Flanagan ;
photographs by Romie Flanagan.

      p.   cm. — (Our neighborhood)

    Summary: Follows an optician as she helps her customers find glasses
that suit them and let them see better.

    ISBN 0-516-20775-X (lib. bdg.)   0-516-26294-7 (pbk.)

    1. Opticianry—Juvenile literature. 2. Eyeglasses—Juvenile literature.
[1. Opticians. 2. Eyeglasses. 3. Occupations.] I. Flanagan, Romie, ill.
II. Title. III. Series: Our neighborhood (New York, N.Y.)

    RE952.F57   1998

    617.7'522—dc21

                                         97-11864

                                             CIP

                                           AC

Photographs ©: Romie Flanagan

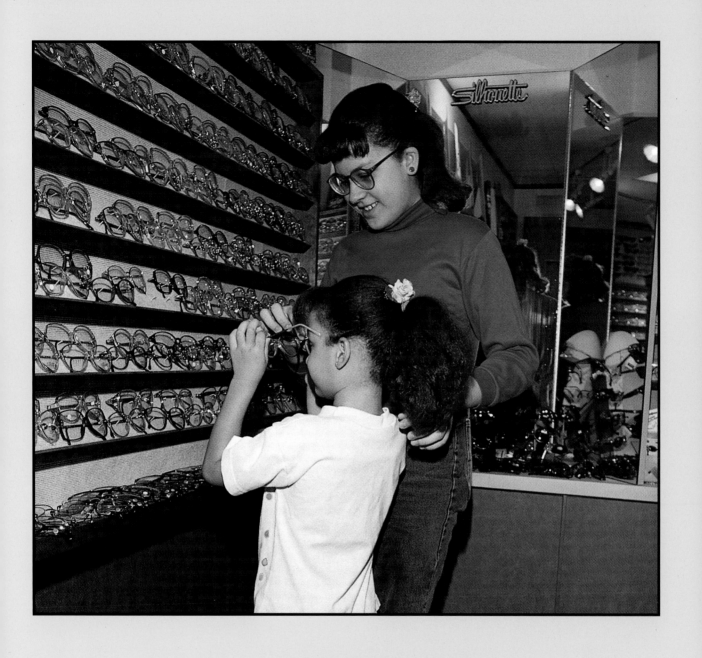

If you need eyeglasses, Mrs. Koutris's office is the place to go.

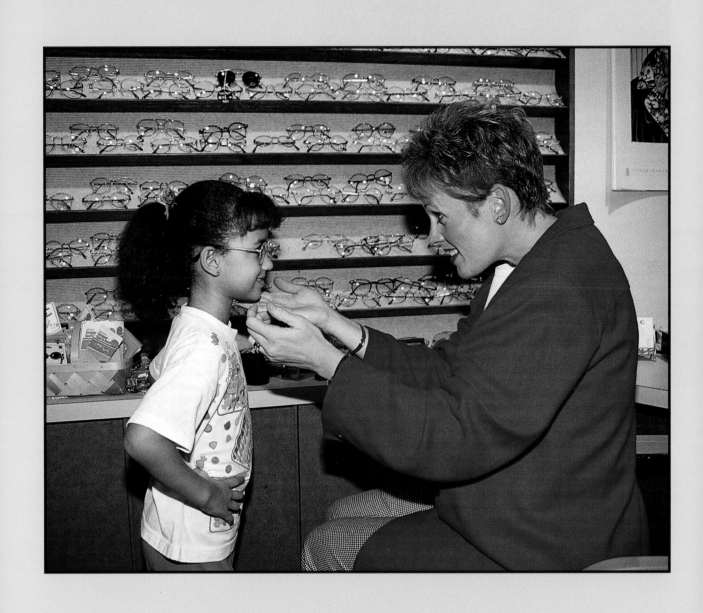

There are hundreds of colorful
frames to choose from.

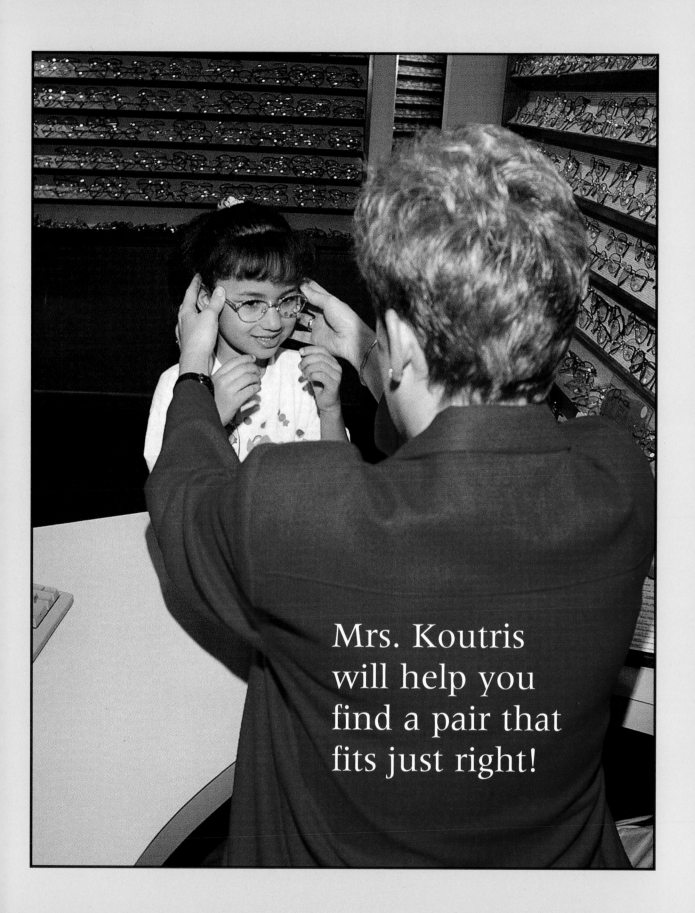

Mrs. Koutris
will help you
find a pair that
fits just right!

Mrs. Koutris is an optician.
She helps people see better.

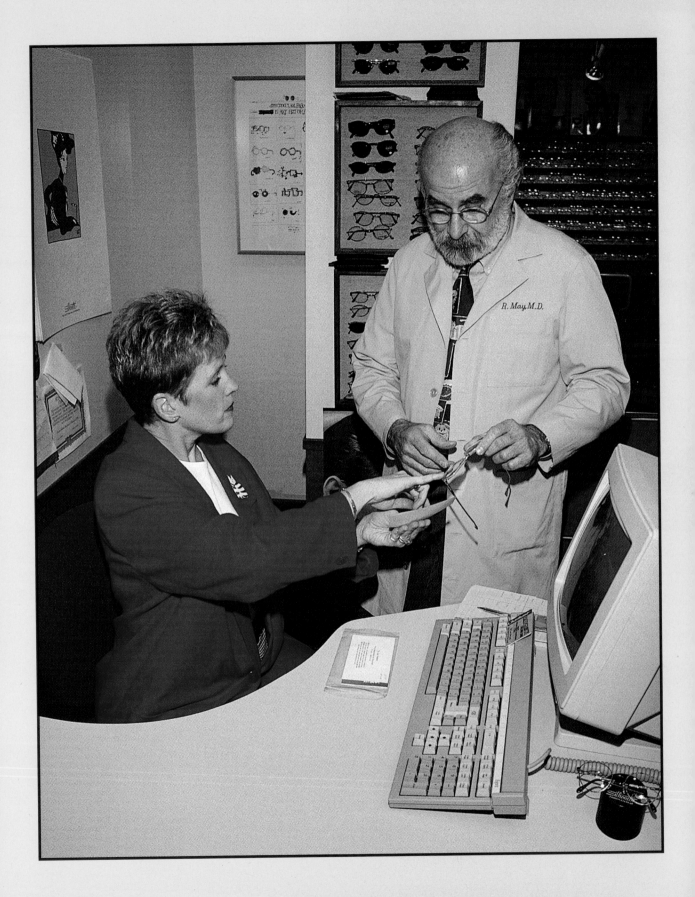

She works closely with Dr. May.
He examines the patients' eyes and
writes down what kind of lenses
they need.

Dr. May's order is called
a prescription.

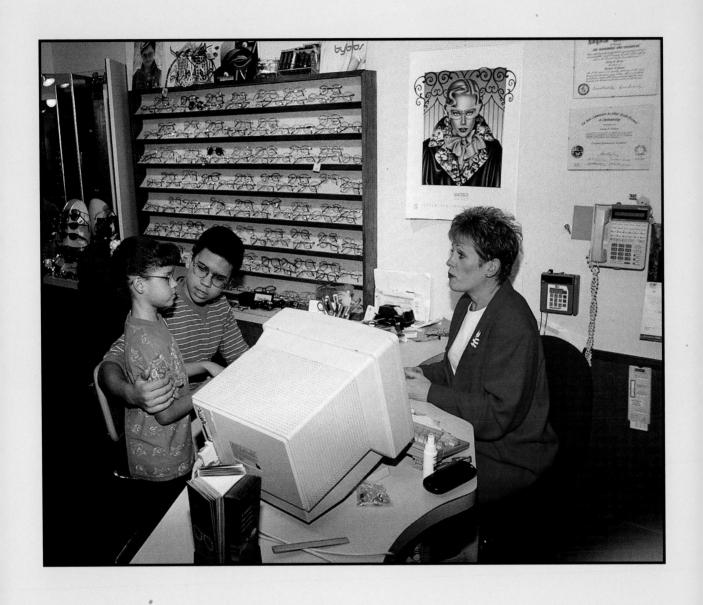

Mrs. Koutris helps patients pick frames that look good on their faces.

Often, people choose frames that are their favorite color.

Sometimes, they pick ones that are a certain shape.

Sports frames should fit nice and tight so they don't fall off during a game.

Mrs. Koutris measures the space between the patient's eyes. She writes down the information.

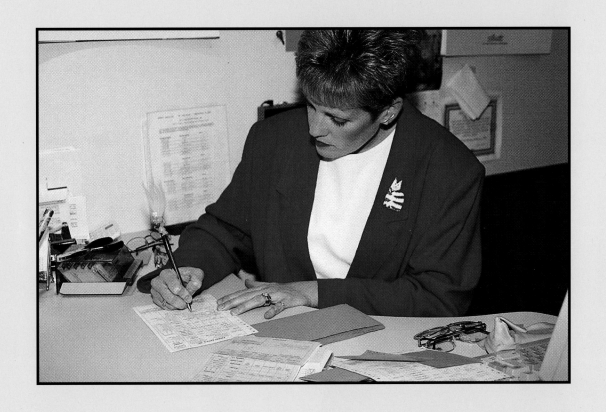

Then, she sends this information
with the prescription and the
frames to the lens makers. They
make the lenses and place them
into the frames.

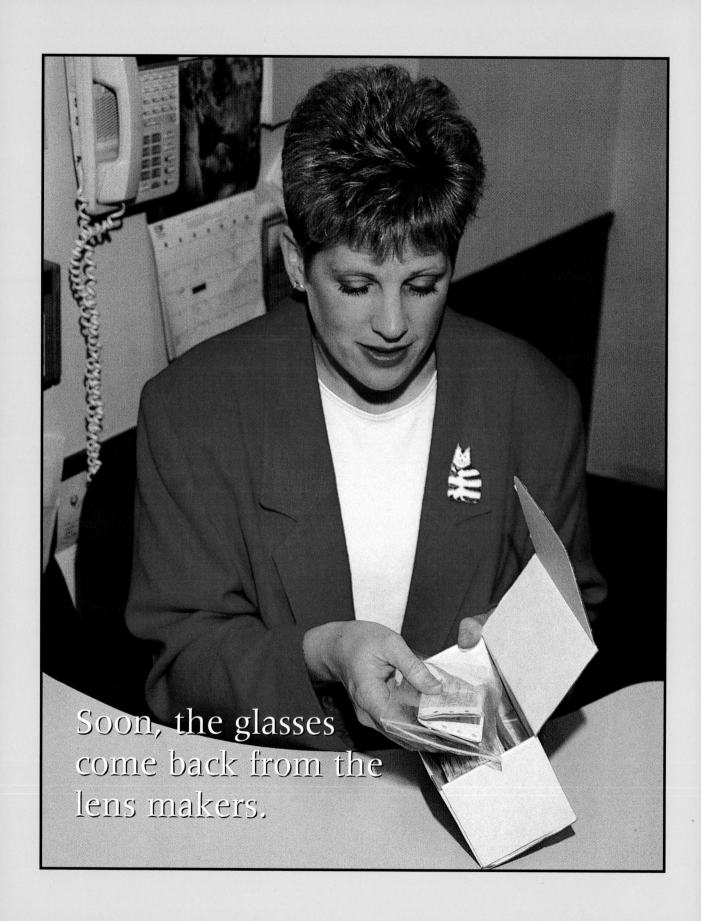

Soon, the glasses come back from the lens makers.

Mrs. Koutris tests the lenses to see if they are correct.

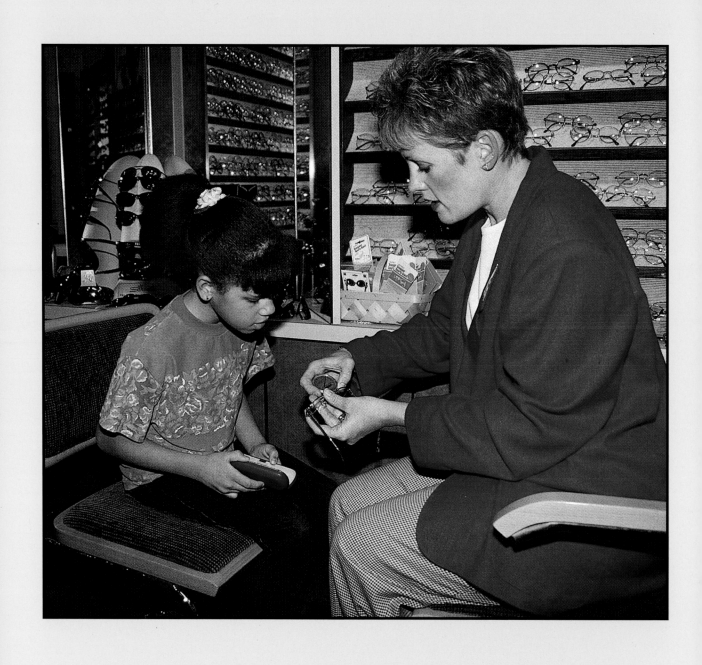

Are they what the doctor ordered?

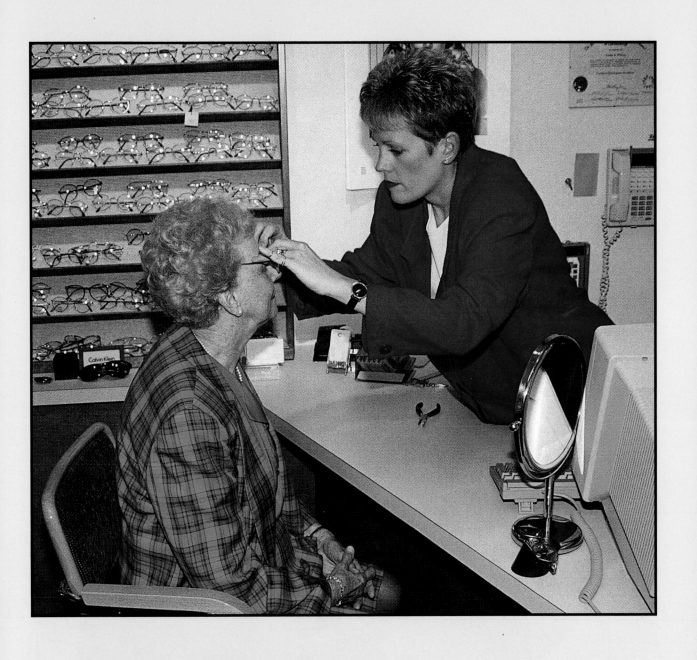

Do they fit in the frames?

Sometimes, she heats the frames

so they can be bent and shaped.

Finally, she tightens loose parts with a screwdriver

and cleans the lenses well.

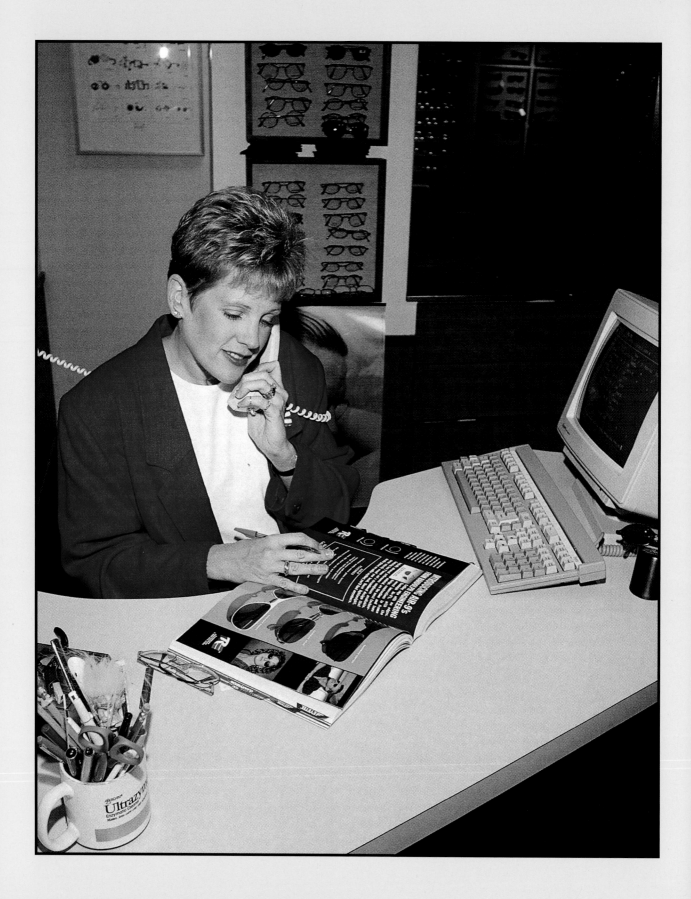

When Mrs. Koutris is not with a patient, she orders supplies

and types information into the computer.

Sometimes, sick or older patients can't pick up their eyeglasses at Mrs. Koutris's office. So Mrs. Koutris brings the eyeglasses to them.

Meeting people is what Mrs. Koutris likes most about her job. She listens carefully to what patients want and helps choose the best eyeglasses for them.

29

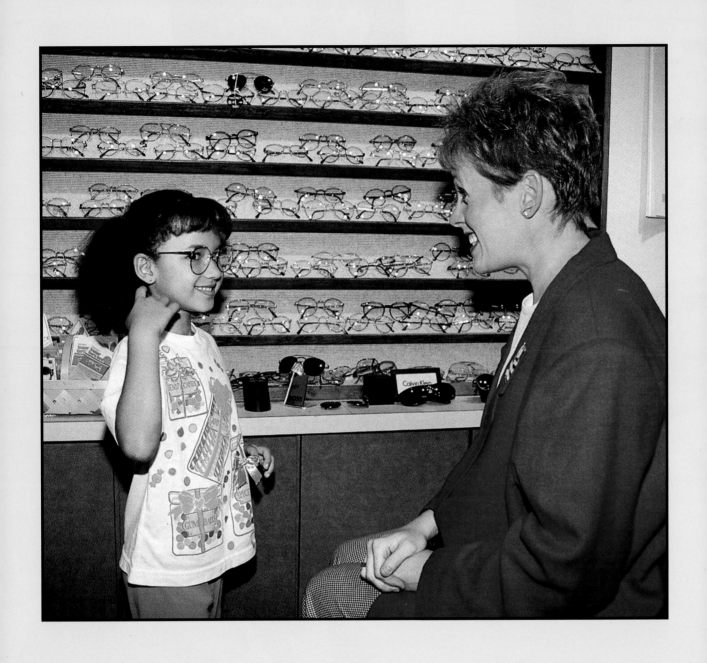

People are happy when they leave
Mrs. Koutris's office.

Because of her help, they can see everything in the world better than before!

Meet the Author
and the Photographer

Alice and Romie Flanagan live in Chicago, Illinois, and have been involved in bookmaking for many years. Alice is a writer, and Romie is a photographer. As husband and wife, they enjoy working together closely. They hope their books help children learn about the people in their community and how their jobs affect their neighborhood.